DISCIPLES PATH
for students

Disciples Path is a series of resources founded on Jesus' model of discipleship. Created by experienced disciple-makers across the nation, it offers an intentional pathway for transformational discipleship and a way to help followers of Christ move from new disciples to mature disciple-makers. Each resource in the series is built around the principles of modeling, practicing, and multiplying:

- Leaders model the life of a biblical disciple.

- Disciples follow and practice from the leader.

- Disciples become disciple-makers and multiply through the *Disciples Path*.

Each study in the series has been written and approved by disciple-makers for one-on-one settings as well as smaller groups.

Contributors:
Heather Zempel, National Community Church in Washington, DC
Josh Howerton, The Bridge Church in Spring Hill, Tennessee
Dr. Craig Etheredge, First Baptist Church Colleyville, Texas
Eddy Pearson, the Arizona Southern Baptist Convention
Dr. Rod Dempsey, Thomas Road Baptist Church, Lynchburg, Virginia

© 2014 Life'
Reprinted Feb. 2016, Jan. 2017

Item: 005737736
ISBN: 9781430041580
Dewey Decimal Classification Number: 248
Subject Heading: CONDUCT OF LIFE \ DISCIPLESHIP \ CHRISTIAN LIFE

Eric Geiger
Vice President, Church Resources

Rick Howerton
Discipleship Specialist

Sam O'Neal, Joel Polk, Karen Daniel
Content Editors

Ben Trueblood
Director, Student Ministry

Chris Swain
Manager, Student Ministry Publishing

We believe that the Bible has God for its author; salvation for its end; and truth, without any mixture of error, for its matter and that all Scripture is totally true and trustworthy. To review LifeWay's doctrinal guideline, please visit *www.lifeway.com/doctrinalguideline*.

For ordering or inquiries, visit www.lifeway.com; write LifeWay Students; One LifeWay Plaza; Nashville, TN 37234-0144, or call toll free (800) 458-2772.
Printed in the United States of America

Student Ministry Publishing
LifeWay Church Resources
One LifeWay Plaza
Nashville, TN 37234-0144

Cover photo and illustrations: Thinkstock

DISCIPLES PATH
for students

Disciples Path is a series of resources founded on Jesus' model of discipleship. Created by experienced disciple-makers across the nation, it offers an intentional pathway for transformational discipleship and a way to help followers of Christ move from new disciples to mature disciple-makers. Each resource in the series is built around the principles of modeling, practicing, and multiplying:

- Leaders model the life of a biblical disciple.

- Disciples follow and practice from the leader.

- Disciples become disciple-makers and multiply through the *Disciples Path*.

Each study in the series has been written and approved by disciple-makers for one-on-one settings as well as smaller groups.

Contributors:
Heather Zempel, National Community Church in Washington, DC
Josh Howerton, The Bridge Church in Spring Hill, Tennessee
Dr. Craig Etheredge, First Baptist Church Colleyville, Texas
Eddy Pearson, the Arizona Southern Baptist Convention
Dr. Rod Dempsey, Thomas Road Baptist Church, Lynchburg, Virginia

Item: 005737736
ISBN: 9781430041580
Dewey Decimal Classification Number: 248
Subject Heading: CONDUCT OF LIFE \ DISCIPLESHIP \ CHRISTIAN LIFE

Eric Geiger
Vice President, Church Resources

Rick Howerton
Discipleship Specialist

Sam O'Neal, Joel Polk, Karen Daniel
Content Editors

Ben Trueblood
Director, Student Ministry

Chris Swain
Manager, Student Ministry Publishing

We believe that the Bible has God for its author; salvation for its end; and truth, without any mixture of error, for its matter and that all Scripture is totally true and trustworthy. To review LifeWay's doctrinal guideline, please visit *www.lifeway.com/doctrinalguideline*.

Unless otherwise noted, all Scripture quotations are taken from the Holman Christian Standard Bible®. Copyright © 1999, 2000, 2002, 2003, 2009 by Holman Bible Publishers. Used by permission. Scripture quotations marked NIV are taken from the Holy Bible, NEW INTERNATIONAL VERSION®. Copyright © 1973, 1978, 1984 by Biblica, Inc. All rights reserved worldwide. Used by permission.

For ordering or inquiries, visit www.lifeway.com; write LifeWay Students; One LifeWay Plaza; Nashville, TN 37234-0144, or call toll free (800) 458-2772. Printed in the United States of America

Student Ministry Publishing
LifeWay Resources
One LifeWay Plaza
Nashville, TN 37234

Cover photo and illustrations: Thinkstock

CONTENTS

A NOTE FOR DISCIPLE-MAKERS

Several years ago I was a part of a massive research study that sought to discover how the Lord often brings about transformation in the hearts of His people. The study became a book called *Transformational Discipleship*. Basically, we wanted to learn how disciples are made. Based on study of Scripture and lots of interactions with people, we concluded that transformation is likely to occur when a godly **leader** applies **truth** to the heart of a person while that person is in a teachable **posture**.

- **Leader:** You are the leader. As you invest in the students you're discipling, they will learn much about the Christian faith by watching you, by sensing your heart for the Lord, and by seeing you pursue Him. I encourage you to seek to be the type of leader that can say, "Follow my example as I follow the example of Christ."

- **Truth:** These studies were developed in deep collaboration with ministry leaders who regularly and effectively disciple people. The studies are designed to take the students you disciple into the Word of God—because we're confident that Jesus and His Word sanctify us and transform us. Our community of disciple-makers mapped out a path of the truths we believe are essential for each believer to know and understand.

- **Posture:** Hopefully the students you will be investing in adopt a teachable posture—one that is open and hungry for the Lord. Encourage them to take the study seriously and to view your invitation to study together as a sacred opportunity to experience the grace of God and the truth of God.

We hope and pray the Lord will use this study in your life and the lives of those you disciple. As you apply the truth of God to teachable hearts, transformation will occur. Thank you for being a disciple-maker!

In Christ,

Eric Geiger
Vice President at LifeWay Christian Resources
Co-author of *Transformational Discipleship*

WHAT IS A DISCIPLE?

Congratulations! If you've chosen to live as a disciple of Jesus, you've made the most important decision imaginable. But you may be wondering, *What does it mean to be a disciple?*

To put it simply, a disciple of Jesus is someone who has chosen to follow Jesus. That's the command Jesus gave to those He recruited as His first disciples: "Follow me." In Jesus' culture, religious leaders called rabbis would gather a group of followers, called disciples, to follow in their footsteps and learn their teachings. In the same way, you will become more and more like Jesus as you purposefully follow Him in the weeks to come. Jesus once said, "Everyone who is fully trained will be like his teacher" (Luke 6:40).

On a deeper level, disciples of Jesus are those learning to base their identities on Jesus Himself. All of us use different labels to describe who we are at the core levels of our hearts. Some think of themselves as athletes or intellectuals. Others think of themselves as musicians, students, leaders, class clowns, and so on.

Disciples of Jesus set aside those labels and base their identities on Him. For example:

- **A disciple of Jesus is a child of God.** In the Bible we find these words: "Look at how great a love the Father has given us that we should be called God's children. And we are!" (1 John 3:1). We are God's children. He loves us as our perfect Father.

- **A disciple of Jesus is an alien in this world.** Disciples of Jesus are aliens, or outsiders, in their own cultures. Because of this identity, Jesus' disciples abstain from actions and activities that are contrary to Him. Peter, one of Jesus' original disciples, wrote these words: "Dear friends, I urge you as strangers and temporary residents to abstain from fleshly desires that war against you" (1 Pet. 2:11).

- **A disciple of Jesus is an ambassador for Christ.** Another of Jesus' disciples recorded these words in the Bible: "Therefore, if anyone is in Christ, he is a new creation; old things have passed away, and look, new things have come. ... Therefore, we are ambassadors for Christ, certain that God is appealing through us. We plead on Christ's behalf, 'Be reconciled to God'" (2 Cor. 5:17,20). Ambassadors represent their king and country in a different culture for a specified period of time. Because we have been transformed by Jesus and are now His disciples and ambassadors, we represent Him to the world through our actions and by telling others about Him.

The journey you are about to take is one that will transform you more and more to be like Jesus. Enjoy! No one ever loved and cared for people more passionately than Jesus. No one was ever more sincere in His concern for others than Jesus. And no one ever gave more so that we could experience His love than did Jesus on the cross.

As you grow to be more like Jesus, you'll find that your relationships are stronger, you have more inner peace than ever before, and you look forward to the future as never before.

That's the blessing of living as a disciple of Jesus.

HOW TO USE THIS RESOURCE

Welcome to *The Beginning*. This resource serves as an introduction for new disciples of Jesus to the core truths of the Christian faith. As you get started, consider the following guides and suggestions for making the most of this experience.

GROUP DISCUSSION

Because the process of discipleship always involves at least two people—the leader and the disciple—each session of *The Beginning* includes a practical plan for group engagement and discussion.

This plan includes the following steps:

- **Get Started.** The first section of the group material helps you ease into the discussion by starting on common ground. You'll begin by reflecting on the previous session and your recent experiences as a disciple. After spending time in prayer, you'll find a practical illustration to help you launch into the main topic of the current session.

- **The Story.** While using *Disciples Path*, you'll find opportunities to engage the Bible through both story and teaching. That's why the group time for each session features two main sections: **Know the Story** and **Unpack the Story. Know the Story** introduces a biblical text and includes follow-up questions for brief discussion. It's recommended that your group encounter the biblical text by reading it out loud. **Unpack the Story** includes practical teaching material and discussion questions—both designed to help you engage the truths contained in the biblical text. To make the most of your experience, use the provided material as a launching point for deeper conversation. As you read through the teaching material and engage the questions as a group, be thinking of how the truths you're exploring will impact your everyday life.

- **Engage.** The group portion of each session ends with an activity designed to help you practice the biblical principles introduced in Know the Story, which are fully explored in Unpack the Story. This part of the group time often appeals to different learning styles and will push you to engage the text at a personal level.

INDIVIDUAL DISCOVERY

Each session of *The Beginning* also includes content for individual use during the time between group gatherings. This content is divided into three categories:

⬆ **Worship:** features content for worship and devotion. These activities provide opportunities for you to connect with God in meaningful ways and deepen your relationship with Him.

➡ ⬅ **Personal study:** features content for personal study. These pages help you gain a deeper understanding of the truths and principles explored during the group discussion.

⬅ ➡ **Application:** features content for practical application. These suggestions help you take action based on the information you've learned as you grow in Christ.

Note: Aside from the reading plan, the content provided in the individual discovery portion of each session should be considered optional. You'll get the most out of your personal study by working with your group leader to create a personalized discipleship plan using the "Optional Activities" checklist included in each session.

ADDITIONAL SUGGESTIONS

- You'll be best prepared for each group discussion or mentoring conversation if you read the session material beforehand. A serious read will serve you most effectively, but skimming the Get Started and The Story sections will also be helpful if time is limited.

- The deeper you're willing to engage in the group discussions and individual discovery each session, the more you'll benefit from those experiences. Don't hold back, and don't be afraid to ask questions whenever necessary.

- As you explore the Engage portion of each session, you'll have the chance to practice different activities and spiritual disciplines. Take advantage of the chance to observe others during the group time—and to ask questions—so that you'll be prepared to incorporate these activities into your private spiritual life as well.

- Visit *Lifeway.com/DisciplesPath* for a free PDF download that includes leader helps for *The Beginning* and additional resources for disciple-makers.

WHAT JUST HAPPENED?

You were created by a passionate God who relentlessly pursued you to bring you into His family. Welcome home.

REFLECT

In this study, we'll explore what it means to be a disciple of Jesus. You're probably reading this because you've recently made a decision to take a step of faith. This decision may seem like something you initiated, but God has been at work in your life and pursuing you for quite some time. Take a moment to describe some of your encounters with God:

Describe the first time you heard about God.

Describe the first time you prayed to God.

Describe a time that God may have been present and active in your life but you didn't recognize it at the time.

PRAY

One of the ways we communicate with God is through prayer. At its core, prayer is simply talking to God—telling Him what's on your heart and actively listening for His response. When you're starting out, it might feel uncomfortable, erratic, and difficult. If so, don't worry. That's normal.

Spend a few moments with God by bowing your head to acknowledge who He is. Close your eyes to block distractions. If you need help getting started, here's a five-point prayer for guidance. We'll be looking at other approaches to prayer in the next few sessions.

- Greet God. How you address God may depend on what you want to talk to Him about. He functions in a limitless capacity: Father, Daddy, Friend, Almighty, Savior, and Redeemer.

- Tell Him what you're thankful for.

- Tell Him what you're concerned about.

- Ask Him to help you understand the elements of the study today.

- Take time to listen for His response.

INTRODUCTION

New creation. Saved. Born again. Redeemed. These are just a few ways the Bible describes "conversion," our response to the great gift of salvation, through which we're forgiven for being less than God created us to be. Jesus called to the disciples, "Follow me," and explained that we must be "born again." But what does "born again" mean?

Ultimately, salvation or to be "born again" means leaving your old ways behind and trusting God. He initiated a relationship with you and offered you a way to experience that relationship. And you responded. That's what just happened to you. You've turned from your old life and turned toward God. You've been freed from sin and made right in His eyes. And you've been rescued from the enemy of God, Satan, and adopted by God.

Read 2 Corinthians 5:17. What old things are you hoping will go away?

What new things do you hope Jesus will bring to your life?

The way we experience God's grace and mercy looks different for different people. Perhaps it felt as though you turned a corner in your life and discovered God right in front of you, or maybe you felt like He chased you down and caught you from behind. Regardless of how you describe your own journey, all such stories share a few things in common—a change in what you believe, a transfer of loyalty, and a reversal of direction. God forgives, saves, restores, and reconciles.

Are there people you've "followed" over the course of your life? There are a few ways you can follow someone or something. You can follow people on Twitter, Facebook, or Instagram. You can follow a favorite sports team or celebrity gossip. You can follow a philosophy or an idea. But when the Creator of the Universe, God in the person of Jesus Christ says "follow me" (see Matt. 4:19), we know intuitively that's something much different.

KNOW THE STORY

One day as Simon Peter was cleaning his fishing nets after an unsuccessful day on the water, Jesus climbed into his boat. Jesus had an unusual instruction for Simon Peter with a miraculous outcome. He told Simon Peter to push back out into the water and to cast out his net again. With much hesitation he did as Jesus said. The net filled up with fish. After the massive amount of fish began to sink his boat, Simon Peter realized who Jesus was and it brought him to his knees.

> [4] When He had finished speaking, He said to Simon, "Put out into deep water and let down your nets for a catch." [5] "Master," Simon replied, "we've worked hard all night long and caught nothing! But at Your word, I'll let down the nets." [6] When they did this, they caught a great number of fish, and their nets began to tear. [7] So they signaled to their partners in the other boat to come and help them; they came and filled both boats so full that they began to sink. [8] When Simon Peter saw this, he fell at Jesus' knees and said, "Go away from me, because I'm a sinful man, Lord!" [9] For he and all those with him were amazed at the catch of fish they took, [10] "Don't be afraid," Jesus told Simon. "From now on you will be catching people!" [11] Then they brought the boats to land, left everything, and followed Him.
> LUKE 5:10-11

What are some practical examples of what it will look like to follow Jesus in your life? (at school, at home, in extracurricular activities, around your friends, etc.)

What will make it difficult to follow Jesus? In what ways will it be easy?

Being a Christian isn't about following rules; it's about following a Person. It's not about asking Jesus to follow us but about deciding to follow Him. Jesus doesn't stand in a far off place and demand that we get our act together before approaching Him; rather, He invades the reality of our lives and invites us into a life larger than our own.

Following Jesus is ultimately about doing what Jesus did the way that He did it. It's that simple. We love the people He loved, serve the people He served, and do the things He did. We strive to imitate His character, ways, and mission.

UNPACK THE STORY

Creation. Fall. Redemption. Re-creation. These four events represent the great story of God—the gospel story. It was the story Simon Peter was swept into and it's the story you have now been swept into. Our lives make sense only as we understand them against this backdrop. Let's examine each of these events.

CREATION—In the beginning, God created. At the sound of His voice, galaxies were hurled into orbit and the smallest organisms were established. Water was pure, creation was untainted, and life was perfect. Then God created man and woman. Fashioned with His own hands and infused with His own breath, He created Adam and Eve to be in relationship with Him and to take care of His creation.

Why do you think it's important to know God as Creator?

FALL—Then, the Villain entered the story. Twisting the words of God and promising a better life, Satan planted a seed of unbelief in the woman's heart. Eve doubted the goodness and trustworthiness of God and reached for the very thing that compromised her relationship with Him. Adam and Eve believed a lie, turned against God, and pursued a story of their own making which left them separated from their Creator. Sin entered the world through humanity and everything broke. And that's what sin is: turning away from God's desire with actions, attitudes, or thoughts.

What effects did Adam and Eve's sin have on the world as they knew it? on their relationship with God?

How do you see sin's effects today?

Violence. War. Dishonesty. Greed. Sickness. Death. God's perfect creation became overgrown with evil, chaos, and despair. It was soon overrun with people who searched for meaning and salvation through selfish ambition. The world needed a Savior.

For centuries, God pursued His people. He gave them leaders, prophets, and priests to guide them into relationship with Him. But over and over, the people became distracted and turned their attention to man-made gods. God's complete redemption was yet to come.

REDEMPTION—In order to reverse the disastrous effects of sin, to free people from the clutches of the Villain, and to restore people to God the Father, Jesus came to the earth with His eyes on the cross. Fully God, Jesus made the perfect sacrifice to pay the debt of our sin and to cancel the curse of death on our lives. Fully human, Jesus was able to fully represent man before God. Redemption had come. On the third day, Jesus rose from the grave to conquer sin and death once and for all.

How was Jesus both fully God and fully man?

Why is this important when it comes to your salvation?

RE-CREATION—The story didn't end at the empty tomb; it had just begun. The great story of God would explode across the globe and change the hearts and lives of men and women for all eternity. All of creation is moving toward a great day when Jesus returns and fixes everything that's broken once and for all.

When you read the overarching story of God, is there anything that surprises you? Explain.

ENGAGE

Here's a simple description of what it means to follow Jesus: doing what Jesus did the way that He did it. Read Philippians 2:5-11 together, aloud. Using this passage as a guide, make a list with the space provided of the attributes and actions of Jesus that His followers should imitate.

Philippians 2:5-11   **Attributes of Jesus**

[5] Make your own attitude that of Christ Jesus, [6] who, existing in the form of God, did not consider equality with God as something to be used for His own advantage. [7] Instead He emptied Himself by assuming the form of a slave, taking on the likeness of men. And when He had come as a man in His external form, [8] He humbled Himself by becoming obedient to the point of death— even to death on a cross. [9] For this reason God highly exalted Him and gave Him the name that is above every name, [10] so that at the name of Jesus every knee will bow— of those who are in heaven and on earth and under the earth— [11] and every tongue should confess that Jesus Christ is Lord, to the glory of God the Father.

PRAYER REQUESTS:

In addition to studying God's Word, work with your group leader to create a plan for personal study, worship, and application between now and the next session. Select from the following optional activities to match your personal preferences and available time.

⬆ Worship

☑ Read your Bible. Complete the reading plan on page 16.

☐ Spend time with God by reading and answering the questions on page 17.

☐ Connect with God each day. Start each morning with the five-part prayer included in the beginning of this study on page 9. At the end of every day, reflect on the times you felt closest to God and when you felt most distant.

➡ ⬅ Personal Study

☐ Read and interact with "How Jesus Came" on page 18.

☐ Read and interact with "Why Jesus Came" on page 20.

⬅ ➡ Application

☐ Connect with your church. Attend a church worship service and take notes as the pastor teaches from the Bible.

☐ Connect with others. Seek out other students who also desire to grow in their relationship with Christ by joining a Sunday School class or small group. Look for an adult to mentor you as you work through your experience of coming into a relationship with Christ.

☐ Memorize 2 Corinthians 5:17: "Therefore, if anyone is in Christ, he is a new creation; old things have passed away, and look, new things have come." Share this newly memorized verse with two different people.

☐ Spend time journaling. Benjamin Franklin said, "The shortest pencil is longer than the longest memory." Keeping a record of the things you are learning and the ways God is working in your life is a great way to track your spiritual growth. Each day, write down one thing you are learning about God.

☐ Other:

⬆ WORSHIP

READING PLAN

Read through the Gospel of Mark this week. Use the space provided to record your thoughts and responses.

Day 1
Mark 1:1-20

Day 2
Mark 1:21-45

Day 3
Mark 2:1-17

Day 4
Mark 2:18-28

Day 5
Mark 3:1-19

Day 6
Mark 3:20-35

Day 7
Mark 4:1-20

HOMECOMING

The first words preached by Jesus are found in Matthew 4:17 where he said: "Repent, because the kingdom of heaven has come near!" It's also the foundation for the first sermon preached in the Book of Acts, when Peter declared: "Repent … and be baptized, each of you, in the name of Jesus Christ for the forgiveness of your sins, and you will receive the gift of the Holy Spirit" (Acts 2:38).

When we hear "repent" we often think it includes punishment or correction. But this word gives life. It doesn't mean "get your act together" or "clean up your behavior" so much as it means to simply turn around: to turn from sin and turn to God. It implies readiness. It results in a complete change of mind, heart, and action, but the first step is to turn around and see God.

> *We don't have to "get our act together" in order to turn to God; we simply turn to Him. What is your reaction to this statement?*

> *Take a moment and read Luke 15:11-24. In what ways can you identify with the lost son? Why do you think his father was so happy at his return?*

This story follows the journey of a young man who strays far from home and far from the man he was destined to be. But eventually he acknowledges his brokenness, turns around, and walks back home. And that's what repentance is. It's homecoming. And when we return home, we don't find a father who is angry or eager to say "I told you so." Rather, we see a Father who runs to us. Jesus doesn't call us to repentance to just change our behavior. He calls us to change our hearts. It's about who or what we are trusting in.

> *Before trusting in the work done by Christ on the cross, what were the things you trusted in?*

The journey home begins with repentance at the cross. The greatest plot twist in history was God Himself coming to earth to deal with sin. At the cross, Jesus took all our sin onto Him and paid our debt. This paved the way for us to go back home. Because of this we know we were created by a passionate Father in heaven who relentlessly pursues His children to bring them back to the family. Welcome home.

> *Give an example of an area in your life in which you need to change direction.*

> *Have you ever thought that your sin was too great for God to accept you? Explain.*

PERSONAL STUDY

HOW JESUS CAME

> For a child will be born for us, a son will be given to us, and the
> government will be on His shoulders. He will be named Wonderful
> Counselor, Mighty God, Eternal Father, Prince of Peace.
> ISAIAH 9:6

God made a promise at the very beginning of time that He would make things right, and that's what the coming of Jesus was about. Jesus came not just to teach moral lessons or to set good examples. He came to liberate, make things right, and start a revolution. Let's look at four of the ways Jesus came to us.

1. Jesus left His rightful place in heaven and came into the chaos of humanity.

In a stone feeding trough for animals, the voice of God was heard in the cry of an infant. He came dressed in the skin of His own creation, subjected Himself to the care of His own creation, and fixed His eyes on the salvation of all people. He showed mercy to sinners. He healed the sick. He commanded dead men to walk out of their graves. He loved and showed honor to the scum of society.

> But we do see Jesus—made lower than the angels for a short time so that
> by God's grace He might taste death for everyone—crowned with glory
> and honor because of His suffering in death.
> HEBREWS 2:9

Have you ever thought of Jesus in these terms? How does the way Christ came to Earth encourage you to live for Him in a culture tainted by sin?

2. Jesus came as a man.

He was born; He had a physical body and physical limitations; He expressed human emotions; He grew physically, emotionally, and relationally (see Matt. 1:18; John 4:6; John 19:28). Because He was fully human, He's able to pay our penalty, to represent us before God, to serve as our example, and to identify with us.

> [7] He emptied Himself by assuming the form of a slave, taking on the likeness
> of men. And when He had come as a man in His external form, [8] He humbled
> Himself by becoming obedient to the point of death—even to death on a cross.
> PHILIPPIANS 2:7-8

3. Jesus also came as God.

His birth was supernatural. He claimed to be God, God declared Him to be God, and even the demons recognized Him to be God. He displayed attributes of deity such as working miracles and forgiving sins (see Matt. 1:18; Col. 2:9). Because He was fully God, He was able to offer a perfect sacrifice.

> And we know that the Son of God has come and has given us understanding so that we may know the true One. We are in the true One—that is, in His Son Jesus Christ. He is the true God and eternal life.
> 1 JOHN 5:20

Is it difficult for you to grasp the thought of Jesus as fully God and fully man? Why or why not?

Why is it important to understand that He is both?

4. Jesus came to serve, sacrifice, and save.

Romans 5:8 declares, "But God proves His own love for us in that while we were still sinners, Christ died for us!" He is uniquely designed to represent people to God and God to people. Because He is fully human, He can offer the sacrifice on our behalf. Because He is fully God, He can offer the perfect sacrifice.

> [9] God's love was revealed among us in this way: God sent His One and Only Son into the world so that we might live through Him. [10] Love consists in this: not that we loved God, but that He loved us and sent His Son to be the propitiation for our sins.
> 1 JOHN 4:9-10

Propitiation is initiated by God. It is His mercy and grace in the form of Christ's sacrifice that makes it possible for us to be in a right relationship with Him. Through Jesus, we experience forgiveness and cleansing.

The Bible teaches that salvation isn't found in what we do for God; rather, it's all about what He has done for us. What is your reaction to this statement?

WHY JESUS CAME

Being a Christian isn't about what you do for God; it's about what God has already done for you. Jesus paid our debt, freed us from sin and death, and reconciled us to God. Jesus divinely disrupted and reversed the story of humanity. On the cross, our guilt, the bondage of sin, and our separation from God was reconciled. During this exercise you're going to unpack these terms for better understanding.

Guilt: Everyone understands words like "guilt" and "debt." But what many don't realize is that we're born into much less-than-favorable standing with God—by association with Adam. We're literally "born into" guilt and bondage. But Jesus paid a debt that He didn't owe and that we couldn't pay so that the charges of sin are canceled against us. Through Jesus, we experience forgiveness and cleansing. This is called *propitiation*.

> He made the One who did not know sin to be sin for us, so that we might become the righteousness of God in Him.
> 2 CORINTHIANS 5:21

How do you typically deal with guilt?

If someone could release you from that guilt, would you let them? Explain.

Bondage: Jesus defeated the power of sin and death on the cross, releasing us from its grip on our lives and offering us eternal life in Him. Through Jesus, we are freed from sin. This is called *redemption*.

> 22 But now, since you have been liberated from sin and have become enslaved to God, you have your fruit, which results in sanctification—and the end is eternal life! 23 For the wages of sin is death, but the gift of God is eternal life in Christ Jesus our Lord.
> ROMANS 6:22-23

In what ways did you feel enslaved to sin before turning to Christ?

Separation: Jesus removed the wedge between us and God and made a way for us to have a relationship with Him. Through Christ, we are reunited with God. This is called *reconciliation*.

> [10] For if, while we were enemies, we were reconciled to God through the death of His Son, then how much more, having been reconciled, will we be saved by His life! [11] And not only that, but we also rejoice in God through our Lord Jesus Christ. We have now received this reconciliation through Him.
> ROMANS 5:10-11

Respond to the following statement: Jesus' work on the cross pays for our sin and removes our guilt. It liberates us from bondage and restores our relationship with God.

Which term do you not fully understand?

Who will you seek out this week to gain a better understanding of this?

Jesus didn't die on the cross to give us comfort and safety. Some people sell salvation like it's an insurance plan or a safety net. Unfortunately, we sometimes think that coming to God means that everything will be OK. Life will get better. Sometimes, it gets worse. We aren't promised that everything will be OK; we're promised His presence. He doesn't promise to keep us safe; rather, He invites us into a dangerous story to share the hope of eternal security in the midst of a very unsafe world.

Jesus didn't die to make us safe but to make us voices of hope in an unsafe world. How might this affect the way you view life?

SESSION 2
CHRIST AT THE CENTER

Christians are people who've had a spiritual revolution placing Jesus at the center of their lives.

REFLECT

We examined in the previous session the overarching story of God and how He has called us into that story. We saw how Jesus' death paid for our sin, freed us from bondage, and restored our relationship with God. We also learned that being a follower of Christ is doing what Jesus did the way that He did it.

Which of the assignments did you explore this week? How did it go?

What did you learn or experience while reading the Bible?

What questions would you like to ask?

PRAY

Begin the session by connecting with God through prayer. Use the following guidelines as you speak with Him:

- Thank God for His goodness and grace in saving you though His Son, Jesus Christ.

- Confess that you are still sinful and need His grace just as much as you did the day you were saved.

- Ask God to bring the hearts of the individuals in your group together over the next few weeks.

INTRODUCTION

The Bible uses a construction analogy to describe followers of Christ, saying that Jesus is our "cornerstone" (see Eph. 2:19-22). For a builder, the cornerstone of a building was central to its construction. It was both the strongest stone and the straightest as every other stone in the building was aligned by it. The cornerstone was laid first. If the cornerstone was straight, every other stone in the building naturally ended up in its proper place. If its angle was even slightly off, every other stone was off. The Bible says Jesus is the cornerstone of a Christian's life. His place in our lives isn't decided by anything else. A Christian is a person who says, "The place of everything in my life is negotiable but Jesus."

A modern analogy would be the universe. Before Copernicus, the universe was interpreted as revolving around ourselves (Earth). Copernicus discovered that something much larger and more powerful was at the center of our universe—the sun—and that everything else revolved around it. This sparked a revolution in which all understanding of the solar system had to be reworked around a new center.

This is exactly what happens when someone becomes a Christian; having realized that Jesus is at the center of the universe, we must rework our understanding of everything else around Him as the new center. This is how everything in our lives finds its proper place. A Christian is a person in the midst of a spiritual Copernican revolution.

What are some fears or confusion you have about life as you know it being reworked around a new center, Christ?

In what ways does the idea of centering everything in your life around Christ bring you comfort and hope?

KNOW THE STORY

The Gospel of Luke describes a man for whom Jesus had become central.

¹ He entered Jericho and was passing through. ² There was a man named Zacchaeus who was a chief tax collector, and he was rich. ³ He was trying to see who Jesus was, but he was not able because of the crowd, since he was a short man. ⁴ So running ahead, he climbed up a sycamore tree to see Jesus, since He was about to pass that way. ⁵ When Jesus came to the place, He looked up and said to him, "Zacchaeus, hurry and come down because today I must stay at your house." ⁶ So he quickly came down and welcomed Him joyfully. ⁷ All who saw it began to complain, "He's gone to lodge with a sinful man!" ⁸ But Zacchaeus stood there and said to the Lord, "Look, I'll give half of my possessions to the poor, Lord! And if I have extorted anything from anyone, I'll pay back four times as much!" ⁹ "Today salvation has come to this house," Jesus told him, "because he too is a son of Abraham. ¹⁰ For the Son of Man has come to seek and to save the lost."
LUKE 19:1-10

What was central to your identity before you became a Christian? What defined you?

Zacchaeus was wealthy because he extorted money from people as a tax collector. But that changed when he met Jesus. Zacchaeus' focus on money shifted (v. 8)—Jesus was the new center of his life.

Why do you think Zacchaeus—a wealthy man by all indications—would choose to give it all up to make Jesus central in his life?

UNPACK THE STORY

CENTRAL TO MY IDENTITY

Zacchaeus was a hated man. For the most part, tax collectors in his time were hated men in a Jewish community for two main reasons:

1. They were notorious thieves who gained their wealth by extorting money from taxpayers. They were hated for their thievery.

2. They were also known as traitors to their culture, as Roman governors would choose Jewish men as tax-collectors in Jewish regions. They were hated for betraying their ethnic community to ally with the pagan Roman government.

Judging from what you know about his story, what do you think Zacchaeus thought about himself before encountering Jesus?

What did Zacchaeus' lifestyle suggest about his identity and motivation?

Zacchaeus had always been hated, but what caused Zacchaeus to change was the whole new view of himself that Jesus gave him: You are loved and accepted by Christ.

Similarly, when we become Christians, Jesus redefines us as He becomes central to our identity and view of ourselves. For Christians, the defining moment of our lives is Jesus' crucifixion on the cross. In that single act, God sealed our true identity: loved and accepted by Christ.

Why is it so important to understand that we are loved and accepted by Christ?

CENTRAL TO WHAT I DO

Jesus must also be central to what we do. He puts everything else in life into its proper place.

The story of Zacchaeus shows that there's only one position Jesus will occupy in a person's life: a central position. When Jesus became central to Zacchaeus, we're shown that it dramatically altered his actions in two areas: people and money.

Because Jesus had become central, Zacchaeus' treatment of people and money were now taking their cues from Jesus. As Christians, we too should try to align every area of our lives with Jesus.

What's difficult about realigning everything in your life with Christ?

What's the most freeing part of approaching life with this new perspective?

Take a few minutes to read Luke 18:18-23. Discuss what you think was going on in the ruler's heart that kept him from obeying Jesus' challenge.

Jesus saw the ruler's heart and asked if he'd be willing to get rid of his money and reorient his entire life. The man went away sad because he didn't want the decisions he made with his money to revolve around Jesus. Because his money was central, the ruler saw Jesus as secondary.

ENGAGE

Take some time to go below the surface and engage the text at a different level. Read Acts 7:54-60 and Luke 23:32-46 together. Circle the similarities you find between how Jesus died and how Stephen died.

54 When they heard these things, they were enraged in their hearts and gnashed their teeth at him. 55 But Stephen, filled by the Holy Spirit, gazed into heaven. He saw God's glory, with Jesus standing at the right hand of God, and he said, 56 "Look! I see the heavens opened and the Son of Man standing at the right hand of God!" 57 Then they screamed at the top of their voices, covered their ears, and together rushed against him. 58 They threw him out of the city and began to stone him. And the witnesses laid their robes at the feet of a young man named Saul. 59 They were stoning Stephen as he called out: "Lord Jesus, receive my spirit!" 60 Then he knelt down and cried out with a loud voice, "Lord, do not charge them with this sin!" And saying this, he fell asleep.
ACTS 7:54-60

32 Two others—criminals—were also led away to be executed with Him. 33 When they arrived at the place called The Skull, they crucified Him there, along with the criminals, one on the right and one on the left. 34 Then Jesus said, "Father, forgive them, because they do not know what they are doing." And they divided His clothes and cast lots. 35 The people stood watching, and even the leaders kept scoffing: "He saved others; let Him save Himself if this is God's Messiah, the Chosen One!" 36 The soldiers also mocked Him. They came offering Him sour wine 37 and said, "If You are the King of the Jews, save Yourself!" 38 An inscription was above Him: THIS IS THE KING OF THE JEWS. 39 Then one of the criminals hanging there began to yell insults at Him: "Aren't You the Messiah? Save Yourself and us!" 40 But the other answered, rebuking him: "Don't you even fear God, since you are undergoing the same punishment? 41 We are punished justly, because we're getting back what we deserve for the things we did, but this man has done nothing wrong." 42 Then he said, "Jesus, remember me when You come into Your kingdom!" 43 And He said to him, "I assure you: Today you will be with Me in paradise." 44 It was now about noon, and darkness came over the whole land until three, 45 because the sun's light failed. The curtain of the sanctuary was split down the middle. 46 And Jesus called out with a loud voice, "Father, into Your hands I entrust My spirit." Saying this, He breathed His last.
LUKE 23:32-46

In what ways was Jesus at the center in each of these passages? How do these passages help you understand what it means for Jesus to be at the center of your life?

In addition to studying God's Word, work with your group leader to create a plan for personal study, worship, and application between now and the next session. Select from the following optional activities to match your personal preferences and avail...

⬆ Worship

- ☑ Read your Bible. Complete the reading plan on ...

- ☐ Spend time with God by reading and answering th...

- ☐ Connect with God each day. Every morning this week, ...s to prayer. Ask God to help you make Jesus central to your identity. Use the ... ... as a starting point. "Dear Father, because of Jesus, there is nothing I did yesterday t... ...e You love me less and there is nothing I could do today to make You love me more."

➡ ⬅ Personal Study

- ☐ Read and interact with "Central to My Identity" on page 32.

- ☐ Read and interact with "Central to What I Do" on page 34.

⬅ ➡ Application

- ☐ Connect with your church. As an expression of the centrality of Jesus in your time, spend time worshiping at your local church this week.

- ☐ Memorize Philippians 1:21: "For me, living is Christ and dying is gain."

- ☐ Do something for someone. Find a practical way to help someone who cannot help you in return this week.

- ☐ Place Jesus at the center. Make a budget and a weekly schedule that reflects Jesus as central to your finances and to your usage of time.

- ☐ Other:

⬆ WORSHIP

READING PLAN

Continue reading through the Gospel of Mark this week. Use the space provided to record your thoughts and responses.

Day 1
Mark 4:21-41

Day 2
Mark 5:1-20

Day 3
Mark 5:21-43

Day 4
Mark 6:1-13

Day 5
Mark 6:14-29

Day 6
Mark 6:30-44

Day 7
Mark 6:45-56

INCREASINGLY CENTRAL

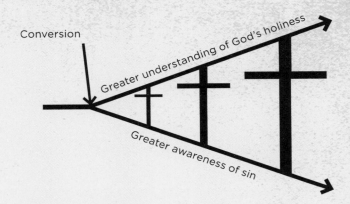

This is a visual representation of the Christian life and the process by which the cross becomes increasingly central in our thinking. The chart moves chronologically from left to right and the point of divergence is when someone becomes a Christian. The longer someone is a Christian, two things happen: they have a deeper understanding of God's holiness and of their own sinfulness.

This is why Paul, one of the holiest men who has ever lived, referred to himself as "the chief of sinners." As these two awarenesses grow, one's view of the cross gets ever larger and larger. Someone who has been a Christian for two decades will be far more aware of how much the cross did for them than someone who has been a Christian for two days. As a person's view of the cross grows, this naturally results in attributes like thankfulness, gratitude, love, mercy, justice, etc. The Christian's character is now being transformed into the image of Jesus. This is a key aspect of how Jesus becomes increasingly central to how we think, feel, and act.

In the time since you've given your life to Jesus, how have you seen Christ become increasingly central in your life?

Do you see the ugliness of your sin any clearer than you did when you first became a Christian? If so, how?

CENTRAL TO MY IDENTITY

In the story of Zacchaeus, Jesus never commanded him to repay those he'd stolen from or to give to the poor. Zacchaeus made that decision on his own. Take a look:

> But Zacchaeus stood there and said to the Lord, "Look, I'll give half of my possessions to the poor, Lord! And if I have extorted anything from anyone, I'll pay back four times as much!"
> LUKE 19:8

What do you think motivated Zacchaeus to do this?

What did Jesus' actions communicate to Zacchaeus about his identity? (See vv. 5-9.)

Is there a moment in your life—a failure, success, etc.—that you have allowed to define you until now? For Christians, the defining moments are Jesus' death for us on the cross and His resurrection. Because of these moments, we find our identity in Him. What once defined us has now been erased and replaced with righteousness, love, and forgiveness.

> God presented [Jesus] to demonstrate His righteousness at the present time, so that He would be righteous and declare righteous the one who has faith in Jesus.
> ROMANS 3:26

> [6] For while we were still helpless, at the appointed moment, Christ died for the ungodly. [7] For rarely will someone die for a just person—though for a good person perhaps someone might even dare to die. [8] But God proves His own love for us in that while we were still sinners, Christ died for us! [9] Much more then, since we have now been declared righteous by His blood, we will be saved through Him from wrath. [10] For if, while we were enemies, we were reconciled to God through the death of His Son, then how much more, having been reconciled, will we be saved by His life! [11] And not only that, but we also rejoice in God through our Lord Jesus Christ. We have now received this reconciliation through Him.
> ROMANS 5:6-11

How do these two passages describe your identity in Jesus?

Look at the following case studies and answer the questions attached to each.

CASE STUDY #1: A young man growing up in a strict, morally conservative family thinks, "I am a good person."

What is at the center of his identity?

What would it look like for this young man to make Jesus central to his identity?

CASE STUDY #2: A teen girl who has been abused and has spent their whole life thinking, "I am dirty."

What would it look like for this young girl to make Jesus central to her identity?

CASE STUDY #3: Someone wrestling with both the gospel and their sexuality says, "I don't know if I can become a Christian because I am gay."

What would it look like for this person to make Jesus central to their identity?

Examine your own story. What are practical things you can do to make Jesus central in to your identity?

➡ ⬅ PERSONAL STUDY 2

CENTRAL TO WHAT I DO

Alarm. Shower. Clothes. Breakfast. Traffic. Tardy. Class. Test. Lunch. More classes. Practice. Locker room. Home. Dinner. Homework. Chores. Text. Bed. Repeat.

What does your day look like? Your life may be shockingly similar to the routine listed above. It may be even more hectic. Life is busy. And it will always be filled with things that compete with Jesus for your attention.

What things in your life are competing with Jesus to be at the center in your heart?

What are symptoms that something besides Jesus is at the center of your life and the decisions you make?

⁵ Trust in the LORD with all your heart,
and do not rely on your own understanding;
⁶ think about Him in all your ways,
and He will guide you on the right paths.
PROVERBS 3:5-6

Read Proverbs 3:5-6 above. Since becoming a Christian, how have you specifically started trusting God? How are you still not trusting Him?

What does it mean to "think about Him in all your ways"?

Take a few moments and examine what it looks like to make Jesus central in the following four areas of your life. Don't hold back. Answer the questions for each area honestly.

FAMILY RELATIONSHIPS:

What are you doing to make Jesus more central to this area of your life?

In what ways are you failing to make Jesus more central to this area of your life?

FRIENDSHIPS / OTHER RELATIONSHIPS:

What are you doing to make Jesus more central to this area of your life?

In what ways are you failing to make Jesus more central to this area of your life?

SCHOOL / ACTIVITIES:

What are you doing to make Jesus more central to this area of your life?

In what ways are you failing to make Jesus more central to this area of your life?

CHURCH:

What are you doing to make Jesus more central to this area of your life?

In what ways are you failing to make Jesus more central to this area of your life?

TIME WITH JESUS

You were created to know God in
a deep and personal way.

REFLECT

We saw in the previous session that Jesus is the central figure in human history and the most important person who ever lived. Jesus is both fully human and fully God, which is why He alone can provide salvation for all people. We also saw that living as a disciple of Jesus means making Him central in all that we are and central in everything we do.

Which of the assignments did you explore this week? How did it go?

What did you learn or experience while reading the Bible?

What questions would you like to ask?

PRAY

Begin the session by connecting with God through prayer. Use the following guidelines as you speak with Him:

- Thank God for His presence in your life this week.

- Ask Him to help you set aside any distractions you're experiencing now so that you can focus on His Word.

- Ask Him to speak with you as you study the Bible today.

INTRODUCTION

We live in a celebrity-obsessed culture. From supermarket magazines to gossip websites to social media, people today are desperate to know what celebrities are up to. We want to know what celebrities are wearing. We want to know which celebrities are dating other celebrities. We want to know where celebrities are dining, shopping, and watching sports. And, more often than not, we've been given round-the-clock access to all of those details and more.

Could it be that at the root of our obsession with celebrities is a desire to connect with something larger than ourselves? As created beings, we're born with an instinctive need to know and be known by our Creator. All of us were created to know God in a deep and personal way.

Don't let that truth slip away: You were created to know God in a deep and personal way.

And here's the wonderful news: You can! You may never have a meaningful connection with a cultural celebrity, but as a disciple of Jesus you have access to something immeasurably better—a daily relationship with the Creator.

God wants to connect with you. He wants you to know Him, come close to Him, hear His voice, and follow His lead.

What is your first reaction to the truth that God wants to know you in a deep and personal way?

KNOW THE STORY

The following story is about two women who knew Jesus personally. Their names were Mary and Martha, and they were the sisters of a man named Lazarus. According to the Gospel of John, "Jesus loved Martha, her sister, and Lazarus" (John 11:5).

Jesus' love for Mary and Martha wasn't a general, unspecific love. It's true that God loves all people, but this was more. Jesus felt a genuine, human fondness for Mary, Martha, and their brother.

One day when Jesus was ministering and teaching near their community, He decided to stop off at His friends' house for dinner. Let's pick up the story there:

> 38 While they were traveling, [Jesus] entered a village, and a woman named Martha welcomed Him into her home. 39 She had a sister named Mary, who also sat at the Lord's feet and was listening to what He said. 40 But Martha was distracted by her many tasks, and she came up and asked, "Lord, don't You care that my sister has left me to serve alone? So tell her to give me a hand."
>
> 41 The Lord answered her, "Martha, Martha, you are worried and upset about many things, 42 but one thing is necessary. Mary has made the right choice, and it will not be taken away from her."
> LUKE 10:38-42

Who do you identify with more in this story, Mary or Martha? Why?

Why was Mary's choice the right choice?

Both Mary and Martha were confronted with a choice between doing what felt necessary and spending time with Jesus. Don't miss the fact that Jesus decided which sister made the "right choice." There will always be things that distract us, oftentimes very good and important things, but Jesus desires our full attention.

UNPACK THE STORY

TALK TO GOD THROUGH PRAYER

As a disciple of Jesus, you have an opportunity to spend time with Him each day. Therefore, like Mary and Martha, you need to make a choice. You can choose to dive headlong into the fast-moving current of your life with all its demands and frustrations—or you can choose to pull back and spend some time communicating with God.

You may be thinking, *How do I communicate with God?* Talk with Him and listen to Him. That's it. That's all you need. Regularly talking with God and listening when He speaks to you are the keys to cultivating a deep and personal relationship with Him.

What are some potential obstacles that might keep you from spending time with Jesus each day?

Prayer is one of the primary ways to talk with God and listen for His voice. People often feel confused about prayer—what it is, what it means, and what it accomplishes. At the core, however, prayer is simply communication with God. It involves speaking to God from your heart and actively listening when He speaks to you.

Notice that prayer isn't a method for approaching God as a genie or divine vending machine. Prayer isn't a way we get God to do what we want. Instead, prayer is the way we draw close to God to find out what He wants.

God draws us close to Himself when we spend time with Him in prayer. For that reason, saturating your life with prayer each day is the beginning step to knowing God and experiencing Him in a meaningful way.

What do you look forward to most when you think about prayer?

What questions would you like to ask about the process and purpose of prayer?

HEAR FROM GOD THROUGH HIS WORD

The more we draw close to God through prayer, the more open we become to hearing and receiving His guidance in our lives. That's why the Bible is so important—because one of the primary ways God speaks to us today is through His Word.

When you read the Bible or hear teaching from the Scriptures, you are hearing from God. The Bible is unchanging, unwavering, unalterable, and always true. Though written thousands of years ago, it has remained both relevant and revolutionary for thousands of years.

In other words, the Bible is God's Word for you today!

What have you heard or been taught about the Bible?

What questions would you like to ask about God's Word?

The Scriptures offer clear principles and practical instructions for life. They are easily understood when studied seriously, and they are applicable for every disciple.

With that in mind, the most important tool you'll need for studying God's Word isn't a commentary or Bible dictionary—it's humility. Just as Mary submitted herself to Jesus by sitting at His feet, you must submit yourself to God's Word by choosing to believe and obey what it says.

As you hear from God through the pages of Scripture and begin to put His truth into practice, you'll continue to develop a deep love and close relationship with Him. In the same way that young children recognize their father's voice, you will begin to recognize and know your Heavenly Father's voice as you study His Word.

What do you hope to experience as you study the Bible?

ENGAGE

Conclude this session by spending time praying together as a group. Use the acrostic PRAY as you follow the steps below. This method of prayer is based on the way Jesus taught His disciples to pray. (See pages 48-49 for a deeper exploration of the PRAY method.)

Note: Groups with more than six participants may want to split into smaller subgroups so that everyone can participate.

- **Praise:** Begin by praising God. Acknowledge how He has shown His love for you in recent weeks. Express your desire to know Him and experience Him.

- **Repent:** Ask God to reveal any habits or unconfessed sins that keep you from knowing Him more deeply. Acknowledge the mistakes you've made and ask for God's forgiveness.

- **Ask:** Actively ask God to meet your needs and to draw you closer to Him in the coming week. Also pray for the others in your group.

- **Yield:** Conclude by yielding your whole self to God. Offer your life to Him this week, and affirm your desire to know Him and be used by Him.

PRAYER REQUESTS:

_____

_____

_____

_____

_____

_____

_____

_____

_____

In addition to studying God's Word, work with your group leader to create a plan for personal study, worship, and application between now and the next session. Select from the following optional activities to match your personal preferences and available time.

⬆ Worship

☑ Read your Bible. Complete the reading plan on page 44.

☐ Spend time with God. Follow the devotional instructions on page 45.

☐ Connect with God each day. Select a time and place to spend focused time with God every day this week—preferably the same time and place in order to begin building a routine. In addition to reading God's Word (see the reading plan), pray about what God reveals to you in your time with Him.

➡ ⬅ Personal Study

☐ Read and interact with "How to Study the Bible" on page 46.

☐ Read and interact with "How to Pray" on page 48.

⬅ ➡ Application

☐ Connect with your church. Attend a church worship service and take notes as the pastor teaches from the Bible.

☐ Connect with others. Ask a friend or family member to join you this week in reading the Bible and connecting with God through prayer.

☐ Memorize John 10:14. "I am the good shepherd. I know My own sheep, and they know Me."

☐ Express yourself. Respond to what you're learning from God and His Word by creating something—a painting, a poem, a song, etc.

☐ Other:

↑ WORSHIP

READING PLAN

Continue reading through the Gospel of Mark this week. Use the space provided to record your thoughts and responses.

Day 1
Mark 7:1-13

Day 2
Mark 7:14-37

Day 3
Mark 8:1-21

Day 4
Mark 8:22-38

Day 5
Mark 9:1-29

Day 6
Mark 9:30-50

Day 7
Mark 10:1-16

INVESTING TIME

If you want to get to know someone better, you have to invest time with that person. The more time you spend together, the more you get to know each other and the deeper your relationship grows. Relationships require time in order to function well.

The same is true for your relationship with God. You were created to know Him in a deep and personal way, but doing so requires an investment on your end.

For that reason, set aside at least 30 minutes to spend with God—and only with God—within the next few days. Choose an environment that feels comfortable for you. This may be in your room with all your devices turned off, or it may be out in the woods with the sun on your face. Either way, intentionally limit this time to praying, studying God's Word, and actively listening for His guidance and direction.

When will I do this? _____

MY THOUGHTS:

➡ ⬅ PERSONAL STUDY

HOW TO STUDY THE BIBLE

Along with prayer, reading the Bible is an essential element for disciples of Christ. The Bible is a miraculous work of literature that has changed the course of human history. It's actually a collection of 66 books written by 40 different authors over a period of more than 1,500 years—yet it tells a single, cohesive story about God and His work in the world. The Bible is the inspired Word of God entrusted to us as a precious gift.

For these reasons and more, the Bible is worthy of our study and attention.

Maybe you're wondering: *How do I go about studying the Bible?* That's a good question, and we can begin finding answers in the Bible itself.

> *Read the following passages of Scripture and write down what they teach about the importance of knowing and treasuring God's Word.*
>
> *Psalm 119:9-16*
>
>
> *1 John 2:3-6*

One of the more difficult concepts to understand about the Bible is how different it is from other books. The Bible is not a spiritual textbook that provides information for living the way Christians are supposed to live. Therefore, reading the Bible should be more than merely an informational experience.

Instead, reading the Bible should be a life-changing experience. The more you study God's Word, the more you should change and grow as a disciple of Jesus. That's what the Bible says:

> For the word of God is living and effective and sharper than any double-edged sword, penetrating as far as the separation of soul and spirit, joints and marrow. It is able to judge the ideas and thoughts of the heart.
> HEBREWS 4:12

> [16] All Scripture is inspired by God and is profitable for teaching, for rebuking, for correcting, for training in righteousness, [17] so that the man of God may be complete, equipped for every good work.
> 2 TIMOTHY 3:16-17

On a similar note, we need to recognize that the Bible was not written the same way other books are written. It's not the product of one person's imagination and experience. Rather, the Bible was written by men who were directly inspired by God's Holy Spirit:

> ²⁰ First of all, you should know this: No prophecy of Scripture comes from one's own interpretation, ²¹ because no prophecy ever came by the will of man; instead, men spoke from God as they were moved by the Holy Spirit.
> 2 PETER 1:20-21

In your own words, describe how the Bible is different from other books you've studied.

For these reasons, one of the keys to studying the Bible is understanding from the beginning that the Bible is literally the Word of God—it's a supernatural book that ultimately comes from God, not from people.

Because of these realities, you should approach the Bible with an attitude of humility and expectation. As you read, use the following questions to help you focus on how God's Word can change your life:

- What principles and truths does this passage communicate?

- What commands and promises do these verses contain?

- What are the implications of this Scripture for my life today and in the days to come?

Finally, remember the words of Jesus as you seek to study His Word:

> ³¹ So Jesus said to the Jews who had believed Him, "If you continue in My word, you really are My disciples. ³² You will know the truth, and the truth will set you free."
> JOHN 8:31-32

How will you change your approach to studying the Bible based on what you've learned in this study?

HOW TO PRAY

You've seen that prayer is an essential practice for those who follow Jesus and want to connect with Him on a regular basis. In fact, prayer is the primary way Christians communicate with God. It's also one of the primary ways we hear Him speak to us.

In other words, prayer is the foundation of our personal relationship with God.

But what does it mean to pray? And how do we actually go about the process of prayer? These aren't questions we should take lightly. Thankfully, we can learn from Jesus' example. While teaching His disciples how to pray, Jesus gave us a model prayer that includes the basic elements we should remember when communicating with God.

Take a look at Jesus' model prayer from the Gospel of Matthew:

> 9 Therefore, you should pray like this:
> Our Father in heaven,
> Your name be honored as holy.
> 10 Your kingdom come.
> Your will be done
> on earth as it is in heaven.
> 11 Give us today our daily bread.
> 12 And forgive us our debts,
> as we also have forgiven our debtors.
> 13 And do not bring us into temptation,
> but deliver us from the evil one.
> [For Yours is the kingdom and the power
> and the glory forever. Amen.]
> MATTHEW 6:9-13

What stands out to you about Jesus' example of how to pray?

How would you describe your experiences with prayer in the past?

You used the simple acrostic PRAY during the exercise on page 42. This is an easy way of remembering the different elements Jesus included in His model prayer.

- **P stands for praise.** Jesus began by praising his Father: "Our Father in heaven, Your name be honored as holy" (v. 9). When you pray, don't rush into your requests and problems. First, praise God for who He is and recognize the positive ways He has worked in your life.

- **R stands for repent.** To repent means to turn from the direction you were going and follow Jesus, instead. Jesus prayed: "Your kingdom come. Your will be done on earth as it is in heaven" (v. 10). Ask God to show you any area of your life where you've ignored or abandoned His will. Confess that to God and turn from it to follow Jesus wholeheartedly.

- **A stands for ask.** Jesus moved into asking for His daily needs in verses 11-13: "Give us … forgive us … deliver us" and more. When you pray, ask God to meet your needs and the needs of others.

- **Y stands for yield.** Some of the later manuscripts of God's Word include the phrase, "For Yours is the kingdom and the power and the glory forever" (v. 13). Jesus was saying: "Father, it's all about Your kingdom, Your power, and Your glory. It's all about You, not about Me." Therefore, close your prayer time by yielding your life to be used as God wants.

It's also important to remember that prayer includes both talking and listening. Even as we open up to God about our thoughts, desires, and fears, we must also listen for His voice in answer. This kind of listening is intentional. It involves setting aside distractions—both internal and external—in order to actively hear what God chooses to speak to our hearts.

How confident do you feel in your ability to listen for God and hear His voice?

Spend a few moments in prayer using the PRAY method described above. How did it go?

SESSION 4
THE BLESSING OF COMMUNITY

Following Jesus may be personal,
but it's never private.

REFLECT

In the previous session, we learned that all people are created to know God in a deep and personal way. This is a tremendous blessing we need to embrace whenever possible. As disciples of Jesus, we have the opportunity and responsibility to connect with God through prayer and through studying His Word.

Which of the assignments did you explore this week? How did it go?

What did you learn or experience while reading the Bible?

What questions would you like to ask before we move forward?

PRAY

Begin the session by connecting with God through prayer. Use the following guidelines as you speak with Him:

- Thank God for the privilege of meeting together as part of a community.

- Be honest with God regarding how you feel about the church, including your past experiences with church and church members.

- Ask for wisdom when it comes to finding your place and your voice in His community.

INTRODUCTION

In the movie *Castaway*, Tom Hanks plays a likable guy named Chuck Noland whose airplane crashes into the Pacific Ocean at the beginning of the film. As the only survivor, Chuck spends the next four years on an uncharted island, isolated and alone.

Chuck's not friendless, however. He finds a volleyball tangled in some wreckage from the plane, draws a crude face on it, and names it Wilson. Then he begins to carry Wilson around the island with him. He engages Wilson in long conversations—even arguing with the ball over important decisions and life-threatening situations.

When Chuck finally builds a raft and attempts to escape the island's reef, he brings Wilson along. And when Wilson is ultimately lost at sea during Chuck's rescue, the man weeps uncontrollably at the "death" of his friend.

Chuck's story is fictional, but it's also a great illustration of an important truth: People were created to live in community.

What emotions do you experience when you're alone for an extended period of time?

Do you agree with the truth that following Jesus was never intended to be a private relationship? Why or why not?

KNOW THE STORY

There are moments in human history that change everything. These extraordinary events mark the beginning of a new era, a new future, and even a new people. God chose to create such a moment 2,000 years ago when He launched the church.

After Jesus' resurrection, He made this promise to His disciples:

> But you will receive power when the Holy Spirit has come on you, and you will be My witnesses in Jerusalem, in all Judea and Samaria, and to the ends of the earth.
> ACTS 1:8

The fulfillment of that promise began weeks later. While Jesus' disciples were praying together, God's Holy Spirit came to them and filled each person with a spiritual power. Inspired by this power, Peter proclaimed the message of the gospel to the people of Jerusalem. More than 3,000 people responded by choosing to follow Christ.

This was a major event in the life of the early church. And how did this new community of believers relate to one another? Check it out:

> [42] They devoted themselves to the apostles' teaching, to the fellowship, to the breaking of bread, and to the prayers. [43] Then fear came over everyone, and many wonders and signs were being performed through the apostles. [44] Now all the believers were together and held all things in common. [45] They sold their possessions and property and distributed the proceeds to all, as anyone had a need. [46] Every day they devoted themselves to meeting together in the temple complex, and broke bread from house to house. They ate their food with a joyful and humble attitude, [47] praising God and having favor with all the people. And every day the Lord added to them those who were being saved.
> ACTS 2:42-47

In what ways is this similar to how believers in your church interact today? How is it different?

Circle the different ways the early church members engaged one another. Which of these do you enjoy most? Why?

UNPACK THE STORY

WHAT IS THE CHURCH?

It's common in today's culture to associate the concept of "church" with a physical structure. When we think about church or about "going to church," we often see images of brick buildings, steeples, sanctuaries, parking lots, and so on.

It's also common for people to think of "church" as something that Christians do. We often make a connection between the church and the practices that are common in church buildings—sermons, worship songs, Sunday School, and more. Each of these associations is understandable, and each does point to the truth. Ultimately, however, the church involves much more.

What comes to mind when you hear the word "church"?

How would you describe your past experiences with church?

In reality, the church isn't a building or a collection of physical structures. Instead, the church is a collection of people. It's a community. In a similar way, the church isn't what we do, but who we are as followers of Jesus.

Here's a definition: The church is the community of people who follow Jesus Christ as Lord.

How is the above definition of church different from or similar to how you would define it?

Every community comes together around specific actions and activities. A community of musicians joins together for the purpose of playing music. A community of sports fans joins together for the purpose of watching games. A community of shoppers cruises the mall together, seeks out specific items for purchase, and enjoys sharing together about great deals and surprising finds.

The community of believers described in Acts 2 also shared common actions and activities. They gathered to learn about God by studying and discussing the Scriptures. They also gathered to serve God and support one another through the ups and downs of life by worshiping together, eating together, praying together, meeting one another's needs, and by making Jesus' love known to the world.

WHAT IS THE PURPOSE OF THE CHURCH?

There are two main purposes for the church:

1. To exist as a community of Christ-followers who support, encourage, and equip one another.
2. To serve as representatives of God's kingdom in order to accomplish His work in the world.

What do you look forward to when it comes to being part of the church?

Both of these purposes are evident in Acts 2. Notice how the members of the church cared for one another: "They sold their possessions and property and distributed the proceeds to all, as anyone had a need" (Acts 2:45).

Because of their love for one another, the earliest members of the church were willing to sacrifice their own possessions in order to meet the needs of others. Such selflessness didn't go unnoticed.

As the early Christians actively showed love to one another and proclaimed the message of the gospel, many outside the church became curious. They wanted to understand what had transformed Jesus' disciples into such caring and compassionate people. In the end, they realized Christ Himself was the source of that transformation. As a result, "every day the Lord added to them those who were being saved" (Acts 2:27b).

What emotions do you experience when you help others? Why?

When have you received encouragement or support as part of a community?

As a disciple of Jesus, there will be times when you find yourself in need of help. In those moments, you'll find support and encouragement within the community of believers—the church. There will also be times when others need your assistance, and you'll find great fulfillment in doing what's necessary to meet their needs as an expression of God's love.

ENGAGE

One of the main purposes of the church is to serve as a community in which disciples of Jesus can both give and receive support when needed. The church exists as a safe place for Christians to encourage and equip one another without fear of judgment or scorn—a place where our actions are guided not by selfishness, but by love.

That's the vision described by Jesus:

> [34] I give you a new command: Love one another. Just as I have loved you, you must also love one another. [35] By this all people will know that you are My disciples, if you have love for one another.
> JOHN 13:34-35

The first step in giving or receiving support within the church is being open and honest with one another. You can't offer prayer and practical support to fellow disciples of Jesus if you are unaware of their needs. Similarly, you won't receive prayer or practical support if you always keep your struggles and challenges to yourself.

Therefore, spend some time as a group discussing the following two questions. The goal of this exercise is not to force you to take on the responsibility of caring for other people. Instead, the goal is to practice sharing the deeper details of your life so that others can know how to offer support.

When have you recently wished for help?

In what areas of life do you currently feel unsure or under-prepared? Explain.

PRAYER REQUESTS:

_____

_____

_____

_____

In addition to studying God's Word, work with your group leader to create a plan for personal study, worship, and application between now and the next session. Select from the following optional activities to match your personal preferences and available time.

↑ Worship

☑ Read your Bible. Complete the reading plan on page 58.

☐ Connect with God each day through times of prayer.

☐ Connect with God by completing the devotional on page 59.

⇒ ⇐ Personal Study

☐ Read and interact with "Two Pictures of the Church" on page 60.

☐ Read and interact with "Two Practices of the Church" on page 62.

⇐ ⇒ Application

☐ Become a church member. Speak with your student minister or Sunday School leader this week about the process and expectations involved with becoming an official member of your church.

☐ Memorize 1 Corinthians 12:27. "Now you are the body of Christ, and individual members of it."

☐ Invite a friend. As you experience the benefits of Christian community, describe those benefits to your friends and invite them along.

☐ Be social. Spend some "hang out" time with another member of your church or group during the week. Invite them over, order pizza, watch a movie, play a game—intentionally enjoy the privilege of being in community.

☐ Other:

⬆ WORSHIP

READING PLAN

Continue reading through the Gospel of Mark this week. Use the space provided to record your thoughts and responses.

Day 1
Mark 10:17-31

Day 2
Mark 10:32-52

Day 3
Mark 11:1-19

Day 4
Mark 11:20-33

Day 5
Mark 12:1-27

Day 6
Mark 12:28-44

Day 7
Mark 13:1-13

WORSHIP ASSESSMENT

Worship is one of the great privileges of participating in the community known as the church. When we gather together as disciples of Jesus, we naturally join together in expressing our devotion to God and our appreciation for everything He has done. This is corporate worship.

For that reason, almost all church gatherings include an element of worship. For example, churches often participate in corporate worship through singing hymns and songs of praise to God. Many churches include additional elements such as visual arts, responsive reading, public testimony, corporate prayer, and more.

This week, take a step back as you participate in worship at your church. Pay attention to how you respond to the worship experience—keep track of your emotions as you worship. Afterward, use the following questions to unpack your experience.

What did you appreciate most about your worship experience? Why?

What did you find confusing or unclear? Why?

How would you describe your efforts to connect with God during worship?

What were some distractions that got in the way of your worship? What might help you focus on connecting with God the next time?

TWO PICTURES OF THE CHURCH

The authors of the Bible often used word pictures to help readers understand difficult or complicated concepts. Let's explore a few examples as we seek to understand the nature and purpose of the church.

First, the apostle Paul identified the church as the body of Christ:

> [12] For as the body is one and has many parts, and all the parts of that body, though many, are one body—so also is Christ. [13] For we were all baptized by one Spirit into one body—whether Jews or Greeks, whether slaves or free—and we were all made to drink of one Spirit. [14] So the body is not one part but many.
> 1 CORINTHIANS 12:12-14

In what ways is the body of Christ like the human body?

Thinking of the church as a "body" is helpful in many ways. It reminds us that no part of the church is more important than the rest—although church leaders are responsible for guiding local churches and serving their members. On a large scale, Jesus Himself is the "head of the church" (Eph. 5:23). Jesus is the brain, and we are the body that exists to obey what He says and do what He wants.

Viewing the church as a "body" also teaches us that we need one another. We are a community of equals gathered into a body. To function well, we must work together. In fact, we must function as a family and remember that God has brought us together according to His plan:

> [17] If the whole body were an eye, where would the hearing be? If the whole body were an ear, where would the sense of smell be? [18] But now God has placed each one of the parts in one body just as He wanted.
> 1 CORINTHIANS 12:17-18

How do these verses help you understand the nature of the church?

How do these verses help you understand your place in the church?

Second, the apostle Peter used several word pictures to describe the nature and purpose of the church:

> [9] But you are a chosen race, a royal priesthood, a holy nation, a people for His possession, so that you may proclaim the praises of the One who called you out of darkness into His marvelous light. [10] Once you were not a people, but now you are God's people; you had not received mercy, but now you have received mercy.
> 1 PETER 2:9-10

Circle the different words Peter used to describe the church.

As with 1 Corinthians, Peter's description of the church reminds us that followers of Jesus have been joined together as a single community. It's true that Christians today are often subdivided into separate denominations or niches. We also gather together in local churches within our specific cities, suburbs, and towns. But at the core, we're all members of God's kingdom.

As members of the church, we are a distinct group of people—a single spiritual community spread throughout every continent on earth.

This reality points to our purpose as the church. Because Christians are connected with one another as a "chosen race" and a "people," we are called to "proclaim the praises" of God (v. 9) and work together to accomplish His will for the world. We have "received mercy" as disciples of Jesus, and we have a responsibility to share that message with others who are in need of mercy as well.

In other words, the blessing of joining together in community as disciples of Jesus should lead us to worship God and tell others about Him.

How do Peter's words help you understand the church's mission?

How do these verses help you understand your role in the church's mission?

TWO PRACTICES OF THE CHURCH

As members of the church, we have the opportunity to participate in a great range of activities intended to help us live and grow as followers of Jesus. These activities include worshiping God, hearing His Word preached, serving others, offering our resources, and so on. These are helpful activities that can benefit us in many ways as followers of Christ.

But let's focus on two specific church practices that help us remember who we are as a community of Christians. The first of those practices is baptism:

> ³ Or are you unaware that all of us who were baptized into Christ Jesus were baptized into His death? ⁴ Therefore we were buried with Him by baptism into death, in order that, just as Christ was raised from the dead by the glory of the Father, so we too may walk in a new way of life.
> ROMANS 6:3-4

What ideas or images come to mind when you hear the word "baptism"? Why?

The practice of baptism involves a new disciple of Jesus being immersed in water as a public declaration of faith in Christ. When the disciple is lowered into the water, it symbolizes his or her death to sin through the sacrifice of Jesus. And when the disciple is raised out of the water, it symbolizes his or her resurrection through Jesus as a new creation and a member of the church.

In other words, baptism is a public symbol and public declaration that a person has been "born again" as a follower of Jesus.

Read the following passages of Scripture. What do they teach about the practice and purpose of baptism?

Matthew 28:18-20

Acts 2:37-41

Acts 8:26-40

The second practice that reveals who we are as members of the church is called Communion—it's also referred to as "the Lord's Supper." Jesus Himself established this practice for the church during the last supper before His crucifixion:

> [19] And He took bread, gave thanks, broke it, gave it to them, and said, "This is My body, which is given for you. Do this in remembrance of Me." [20] In the same way He also took the cup after supper and said, "This cup is the new covenant established by My blood; it is shed for you."
> LUKE 22:19-20

Different churches practice the Lord's Supper in different ways, but the basic elements are the same. Within the community of the church, disciples of Jesus obey His command by eating and drinking in order to remember His sacrifice on our behalf.

How would you describe your past experiences with the Lord's Supper?

What questions do you have about the practice of the Lord's Supper?

The practice of the Lord's Supper is vital because it reminds us of the nature of the church. Throughout the world and throughout the history of the church, disciples of Jesus have been linked together through the Lord's Supper. It helps unite us as a community.

In the same way, the Lord's Supper reminds us of the church's purpose. Even as we commemorate the death of Jesus as the payment for our sins, we're reminded that others need to experience His forgiveness. The Lord's Supper inspires us to share the gospel message with a world still in need of a Savior.

Now that you've learned about baptism and the Lord's Supper, what's your next step as a follower of Jesus?

SESSION 5
JOINING JESUS ON MISSION

Disciples are called to know Christ, grow
with Christ, and go for Christ.

REFLECT

As we learned in the previous session, living as a disciple of Jesus is a deeply personal matter that must also be expressed in a public way. People are designed to live in community, which is why participation in the church—the community of people who follow Jesus Christ as Lord—is an essential part of following Jesus.

Which of the assignments did you explore this week? How did it go?

What did you learn or experience while reading the Bible?

What questions would you like to ask before moving forward?

PRAY

Begin the session by connecting with God through prayer. Use the following guidelines as you speak with Him:

- Thank God for creating the church and for giving you a community of believers you can worship alongside.

- Ask God to give you an understanding of and a passion for His mission in the world.

- Ask for wisdom as you study what it means to join the church in working to achieve Christ's mission for the world.

INTRODUCTION

"Soldiers, sailors and airmen of the Allied Expeditionary Force! You are about to embark upon the Great Crusade, toward which we have striven these many months. The eyes of the world are upon you. The hopes and prayers of liberty-loving people everywhere march with you."[1]

These were the opening words of General Dwight D. Eisenhower when he sent the orders launching the D-Day invasion of June 6, 1944, near the end of World War II. Until that day, the Axis forces led by Germany held Europe in an iron grip of oppression and tyranny. The situation was grim. The world was waiting.

Thankfully, we know the rest of the story. The landing of Allied forces on the beaches of Normandy essentially turned the tide of the war. Less than a year later, Germany surrendered.

In a similar way, Jesus' life, death, and resurrection forever changed the course of human history. Although Jesus didn't use an army to achieve His victory over sin, He did launch the church—an ever-increasing, always-expanding movement of disciples.

As a follower of Christ, you're part of that movement. Therefore, you're called to participate in His continuing mission for the world. That mission contains several different elements, but they can all be boiled down to a core assignment: making disciples of Jesus Christ.

How do you feel about being included as a member of the movement called the church?

What emotions do you experience at the thought of telling others about Jesus?

1. Jonathan Foreman, *The Pocket Book of Patriotism*, (New York: Sterling Publishing Co., Inc., 2005), 75.

KNOW THE STORY

Jesus talked often about His mission for the world. But His most memorable descriptions of that mission were connected with His first and last words to the disciples. The first came when He called the disciples to follow Him.

In Session 1 we explored this story from the perspective of choosing to follow Jesus. Now let's focus on Jesus' larger mission for the world:

> ¹⁸ As He was walking along the Sea of Galilee, He saw two brothers, Simon, who was called Peter, and his brother Andrew. They were casting a net into the sea, since they were fishermen. ¹⁹ "Follow Me," He told them, "and I will make you fish for people!" ²⁰ Immediately they left their nets and followed Him.
> MATTHEW 4:18-20

Jesus' mission for His disciples can be boiled down to two simple phrases: "follow Me" and "fish for people."

What have you learned about the process of following Jesus? What does this have to do with "fishing for people"?

After His death and resurrection, Jesus confirmed and expanded His mission during one of His final conversations with the disciples:

> ¹⁸ Then Jesus came near and said to them, "All authority has been given to Me in heaven and on earth. ¹⁹ Go, therefore, and make disciples of all nations, baptizing them in the name of the Father and of the Son and of the Holy Spirit, ²⁰ teaching them to observe everything I have commanded you. And remember, I am with you always, to the end of the age."
> MATTHEW 28:18-20

How confident do you feel about obeying Jesus' commands in these verses? Why?

UNPACK THE STORY

YOUR MISSION IS FROM JESUS

Jesus words from Matthew 28:18-20 are often referred to as the Great Commission. They summarize what Jesus commissioned, or sent, His disciples to do. And because Jesus extended the mission "to the end of the age" (v. 20), His words apply to all His disciples throughout history—including you.

As a new disciple of Christ, you are part of Jesus' continuing mission for the world. What's more, as a new disciple, you are called to participate in that mission by helping to make more disciples of Christ.

Does the idea of "making disciples" scare you or excite you? Explain.

With that in mind, remember that the foundation of Jesus' commission was His own authority. Jesus said: "All authority has been given to Me in heaven and on earth" (v. 18). In other words, He wanted everyone to understand that He's in charge of everything connected to this world—and beyond.

Why is that important? Because a mission is only as good as the person (or Person) commanding it.

If a regular soldier had sent out the order to attack on D-Day, nobody would have paid attention. But since the orders came instead from the general in command, they had weight. They carried authority that demanded obedience.

In the same way, Jesus is the most important person who ever lived. His life, death, and resurrection are the central moments in human history, and He exists as both God and man. Therefore, His words demand obedience from us.

How does knowing that Jesus has all authority help you obey Him?

YOUR MISSION IS TO MAKE DISCIPLES

The core of Jesus' statement from the Great Commission is "make disciples of all nations" (v. 18). But how do we do that? What does it look like to make disciples? Where do we get started, and what are we supposed to do?

Fortunately, Jesus offered three practical steps we can follow in order to make new disciples in His Name:

- **Go:** You can't just sit around and expect to make disciples. Jesus commanded us to go to our family members, go to our friends, go into our communities, and even go throughout the world as we proclaim the gospel.

- **Baptize:** To be baptized is to make a public declaration of faith in Jesus Christ. This helps us remember our mission isn't to get people to stop sinning, or even to convince them to attend church. Our mission is to proclaim the good news of Jesus Christ and help others confess Him as Lord.

- **Teach:** The process of making a disciple doesn't end at declaring belief in Christ. When someone experiences salvation, we're called to teach them to observe everything Jesus commanded. In other words, we have a responsibility to teach new disciples what it means to live as a disciple of Christ.

Which of the above steps seems most difficult to you? Why?

Which of these steps have you experienced already? Explain.

The process of making disciples for Jesus is called discipleship. And it is a process—it takes time. In fact, you will never be "finished" as a disciple of Jesus. You will always have room to grow and mature.

Therefore, be patient with yourself. And be patient with those you invite to walk with you as you begin this process of making disciples.

ENGAGE

Sharing your testimony—your story of experiencing salvation and choosing to follow Jesus—will be one of your most effective tools for making disciples. Many Christians feel nervous at the thought of sharing their testimony, but doing so doesn't have to be a frightening or frustrating experience. Nor does it need to be confrontational.

Instead, simply talk through your answers to the following questions:

How would you describe your life before you encountered Jesus?

How did you come to know and follow Jesus?

What changes have you experienced since becoming a disciple of Jesus?

Telling your story can be a powerful experience—both for you and for those who hear you. As time allows, practice sharing your testimony with the members of your group. Use this experience to gain insight and feedback so you can be ready when the time comes for you to share the good news of salvation with someone who needs to hear it.

PRAYER REQUESTS:

_____

_____

_____

_____

_____

_____

_____

_____

In addition to studying God's Word, work with your group leader to create a plan for personal study, worship, and application. Select from the following optional activities to match your personal preferences and available time.

⬆ Worship

☑ Read your Bible. Complete the reading plan on page 72.

☐ Connect with God by praying about your place in His mission for the world. Ask God to show you opportunities to help make disciples each day.

☐ Spend time with God by completing the devotional on page 73.

➡ ⬅ Personal Study

☐ Read and interact with "Your Mission Is for the World" on page 74.

☐ Read and interact with "Your Mission Includes the Church" on page 76.

⬅ ➡ Application

☐ Go for it. Share your testimony this week with at least one person who needs to experience what Jesus has to offer.

☐ Memorize John 14:6: "Jesus told him, 'I am the way, the truth, and the life. No one comes to the Father except through Me.'"

☐ Look to your community. Meet with your student minister or work with your small group or Sunday School leader to determine specific ways you can spread the message of the gospel within your local community.

☐ Look to the ends of the earth. Research organizations such as World Changers and P2 Missions currently working to spread the gospel. Ask your student minister about international missions opportunities available through your local church.

☐ Other:

↑ WORSHIP

READING PLAN

Continue reading through the Gospel of Mark this week. Use the space provided to record your thoughts and responses.

Day 1
Mark 13:14-37

Day 2
Mark 14:1-26

Day 3
Mark 14:27-52

Day 4
Mark 14:53-72

Day 5
Mark 15:1-20

Day 6
Mark 15:21-47

Day 7
Mark 16:1-8